# DAVID DALE, ROBERT OWEN — AND THE STORY OF — NEW LANARK

## CONTENTS

in association with

MOUBRAY HOUSE PUBLISHING
Tweeddale Court
14 High Street, Edinburgh EH1 1TE
Telephone 031-557 3349

NEW LANARK CONSERVATION
No. 3 Mill
New Lanark ML11 9DB
Telephone Lanark 61345

*Society of Friends Library), Dorothy Steedman and Anne Whitaker.*
*David Willis of Crichton Lang, Willis and Galloway, Architects (successors to Ian Lindsay and Partners), who have contributed so much to the restoration of New Lanark, kindly allowed the use of his magnificent axonometric view of the village.*
*The John Winning watercolours are reproduced by kind permission of John Hume, Dr and Mrs R. H. L. Cohen, Mrs Fern Lyon and Mr Neil Wallace.*
*Other illustrations are reproduced by kind permission of:*
*Royal Commission on the Ancient and Historical Monuments of Scotland (p. 8, 9, 11, 12, 19, 20, 34).*
*National Galleries of Scotland (p. 5, 7)*
*Edinburgh University Library (p. 16).*
*Bridon Ropes Ltd. and Glasgow University Library (p. 1, 5, 8, 17, 31).*
*Glasgow Herald (p. 35).*
*Scotsman Publications Ltd. (p. 39).*
*Mansell Collection (p. 16).*

*Other illustrations provided by New Lanark Conservation.*

*Colour photography by Nic Allen.*

*Books to Read:*

*David McLaren: David Dale of New Lanark (1983).*
*Frank Podmore: Robert Owen (1906).*
*John Butt (ed): Robert Owen, Prince of Cotton Spinners (1971).*
*Includes an extensive essay on the Industrial Archaeology of New Lanark by John Hume.*

Text: Nic Allen
Managing Editor: Sheila Mackay
Sub-editor: Jeremy Bruce-Watt
Advertising Associate:
Margaret Wilson
Design: Graphic Partners
ISBN 0 948473 02 9

2nd Edition 1989

# INTRODUCTION

A few miles upstream of Lanark, the Clyde changes both its direction and its character. The river which has meandered through the rolling hills of upper Clydesdale disappears into a dramatic gorge and becomes a roaring torrent. The foaming whiteness of the rushing water and the greenery of the trees and bushes which tumble down to the river's edge set a scene of remarkable beauty. Every few yards along the riverside path a new and more picturesque view opens up to reveal another cataract or waterfall, or an eddy coated with dappled shadows where the sun shines through the leaves onto the water.

A final turn on the footpath brings into view a man-made scene to compare with the beauties of nature around it. Passing through an opening in an ivy-covered wall the visitor might feel he has also come through a time-warp, for in front of him lies a substantial settlement, little changed since the closing years of the eighteenth century. New Lanark possesses little of the softness of older rural communities. It has the hard, classical, even urban, beauty of the early Industrial Revolution. The visitor, whether approaching by this route or, as most do, by way of Lanark (from which both Edinburgh and Glasgow are less than an hour's drive away) experiences much the same feelings that William Blake must have had when confronted, in the depths of the green and gentle countryside, with his first sight of the 'dark Satanic Mills'.

A virtually intact eighteenth century village set in beautiful countryside; this combination by itself would make New Lanark a remarkable attraction. But this does not even touch on the real fascination of the place. What makes New Lanark unique is that it was here, in the early years of the nineteenth century, that Robert Owen, building on the enterprise of David Dale, his father-in-law and the founder of the village, commenced what he confidently asserted was "the most important experiment for the happiness of the human race that has yet been instituted at any time in any part of the world".

New Lanark was to become the model for an industrial society in which compassion and commerce flourished hand-in-hand. Many of the later policies of Owen and his fellow-reformers were to lead straight down an historical cul-de-sac. New Lanark did not. It was here, deep in the Clydesdale countryside, that social and economic ideas were first developed which today have become commonplace from Stockholm to San Francisco to Tokyo.

# VALLEY OF BEAUTY, VILLAGE OF CHILDREN

A day in 1783 found two stout, middle-aged men, one Scots the other English, tramping the banks of the River Clyde just south of the county town of Lanark. Appreciation of the already well-known beauties of the area was clearly not their major interest but they were as excited as any sightseers by what they found. The Englishman – none other than Richard Arkwright, the inventor and pioneer of industrial cotton-spinning – declared that no other place in Scotland afforded "more eligible situations for mills of all kinds", and prophesied that in time Lanark would become the Manchester of Scotland. His companion, the Glasgow banker and entrepreneur, David Dale, obviously agreed. Within a year he and Arkwright had formed a partnership and purchased a riverside tract – "a mere morass situated in a hollow den and of difficult access" – from the local landowner, Lord Justice Clerk Braxfield, the notorious "hanging judge". They then began the construction of what was to become the most famous cotton-spinning community in the country. They called it "New Lanark".

## HARNESSING THE CLYDE

The very qualities which made the Clyde so picturesque at this point – a torrent of water rushing headlong down a narrow gorge – now made it an ideal site for water-driven spinning mills. Arkwright was foremost among those who realised that water-powered mechanisation of spinning was capable of bringing improvements in production which were quite staggering to people hitherto accustomed to the sight of the woman at her spinning wheel. The new machines, driven by a single giant water-wheel, could do the work of literally thousands of individual wheels. The operation of giant wheels, however, demanded large, rapidly flowing rivers and, to the frustration of the pioneers of water-powered mechanisation, these were a rarity in central Scotland where rivers tend to be either large and slow or small and fast. The Clyde at Lanark was a happy exception and so, just as our oil-powered economy has been prepared to search the distant and inhospitable depths of the North Sea to find its sources of energy, Dale and Arkwright determined to overcome problems of access to Lanark and the appalling road from there to Glasgow and sited what was to become the largest cotton-spinning mill in Britain, deep in rural Clydesdale.

Once the site for New Lanark had been purchased, development was rapid. Dale dissolved his partnership with Arkwright in 1785 and as sole proprietor continued building without interruption. The first mill was begun in April, 1785, and although the twists and turns of the Clyde meant that a weir had to be built upstream and water channelled from there to the mills by means of a thousand foot tunnel cut through solid rock, spinning began in March, 1786. Work began on a second mill two years later but within a month, on 9th October, 1788, the first mill burned to the ground. Dale's masons and millwrights were kept busy in the years that followed completing the second (No. 2) mill, replacing the first (No. 1) and building two further mills.

By 1793 the clatter of water-driven machinery echoed through New Lanark. In No. 2 mill three water-wheels were driving 6000 spindles. In No. 1, which had not yet resumed full production after the fire, some 4500 spindles were at work. In No. 3 mill the spindles were operated by 55 "common" jennies as well as a considerable number of "patent" jennies – the invention of William Kelly whom Dale had appointed as his manager. The latest and largest mill, No. 4, provided workshops, storage and accommodation. The noise in the mill workrooms, each up to 150 feet long and 30 feet wide, can well be imagined. In addition to the inevitable din of the machinery driving 2000-odd spindles, there would be the bustle of 50 to 75 workers.

## NEW LANARK'S GREATEST ASSET: CHILDREN

What would have pulled the modern observer up short was the nature of the workforce. New Lanark, by now the largest single industrial enterprise in Scotland, was predominantly operated by children. Of the 1157 people employed there in spinning in 1793, 362 were adults but nearly 800 were young boys and girls. Of these, 450 were not even in their teens and included 95 nine-year-olds, 71 eight-year-olds, 33 seven-year-olds and even five six-year-olds. It is small wonder that schooling was to play such an important part in the social reforms of both Dale and Owen.

The difficulties of bringing together this considerable workforce (another 87 were employed in related mill trades as smiths, millwrights, founders, etc.) in rural eighteenth century Scotland are not to be underestimated. Dale drew initially on Lanark, the surrounding parishes and the orphanages of Edinburgh and Glasgow who supplied children on the basis that Dale

| | | |
|---|---|---|
| | ,, | Mr R. Goodall, of Lisbon |
| | ,, | Mr & Mrs Douglas Portld place Lond. |
| | | Mr Williamson |
| | 12 | Alexr Brown Edinr |
| | ,, | George Newton Edinr |
| | ,, | John Forbes Edinr |
| | ,, | Alexr Nasmyth Landskip painter Edinr |
| | ,, | Mrs Forbes |
| | ,, | Mrs Nasmyth |
| 314 | ,, | Mr & Mrs Loban & Mrs Alexander Glas |
| | 14 | [illegible] Glasgow |
| | ,, | Ann [illegible] |
| 347 | | Margaret Lawson |

"As you come nearer you are most agreeably surprised in seeing a most extraordinary cataract of the whole river . . . the high rocks on each side are most beautifully adorned with trees, being altogether the finest cascade I ever saw."—Richard Pococke, 'Tours in Scotland, 1760.

Long before Dale and Arkwright visited what was to become the site of New Lanark, the Falls of Clyde were famed for their romantic beauty. Jacob More first exhibited his painting of Corra Linn (above), now in the National Gallery of Scotland, in 1771. Other artists attracted to the Falls included Turner and Alexander Nasmyth, who left a record of his visit in David Dale's New Lanark Visitors Book.

*"When George(III) ascended the throne . . . thread was spun on the single wheel . . . the spinner, with the utmost exertion, producing but a few hanks by a day's labour. Ere he died that same King, had he passed through his British dominions might have found nearly half-a-million engaged, in vast factories, in spinning and manufacturing cotton; each spindle turning out, on the average, some three hundred times as much yarn as before. A century ago, it would have required the manual labour of one-third of the population of the world to supply as much cotton yarn as is turned out today by the cotton mills of Great Britain alone."—Robert Dale Owen, Threading My Way.*

*The skill of the hand spinner lay in the ability to draw out a strand of pre-carded cotton to just the right tautness (and thus thickness) at which it could be twisted onto a bobbin by a rotating U-shaped "flyer" powered by the foot-driven wheel. The secret of Arkwright's much disputed patent (below), was the series of geared rollers at the top of the spinning frame which mechanically imitated the action of the hand spinner, drawing out the thread (or "rovings") from large bobbins behind the frame through four pairs of rollers, each geared so that the rovings passed from slower to faster-moving rollers (the speeds increasing in a ratio 1:1.17:1.33:6.25) and so pulled tighter and tighter.*

*The gearing mechanism was not dissimilar to that turning different hands at varying speeds in a clock and, indeed, it was with a clockmaker, John Kay, that Arkwright collaborated to produce his machine. The same power source which operated the rollers also operated the flyer which twisted the thread on to the bobbin. No longer did every roving need to be drawn out by an individual spinner — a handful of relatively unskilled workers could supervise machines, spinning*

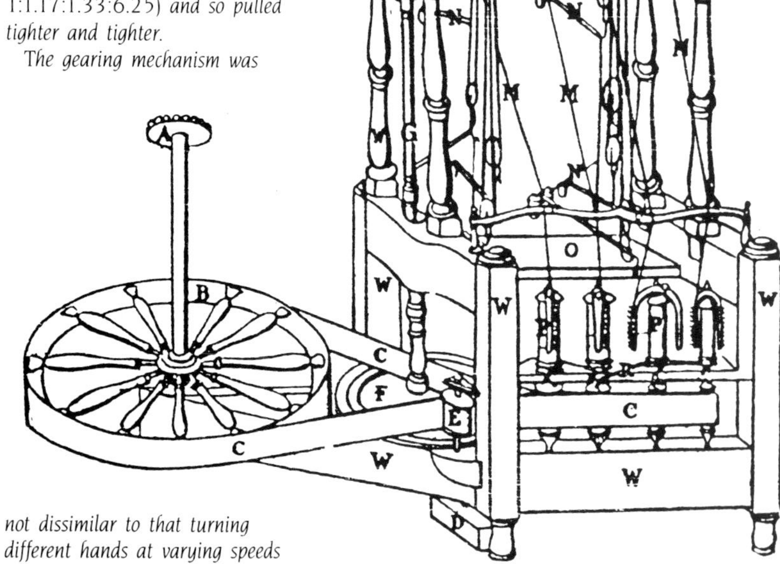

would provide for their maintenance in lieu of the wages which the children of village families received. The dormitory in No. 4 mill was home to these orphans.

Harsh though the use of child labour might seem to us, it was quite normal in eighteenth century Britain. What contemporaries remarked upon was not Dale's employment of children but just how well he treated the orphans by the standards of the time. In 1796, David Dale in reply to the Manchester Board of Health, reported that the dormitories accommodated 396 boys and girls.

*"There are six sleeping apartments for them, and three children are allowed to each bed. The ceilings and walls of the apartments are whitewashed twice a year with hot lime and the floors washed with scalding water and sand. The children sleep on wooden-bottomed beds on bed ticks filled with straw which is in general changed once a month. A sheet covers the bed ticks and above that there are one or two pairs of blankets and a bed cover as the season requires. The bedrooms are carefully swept and the windows thrown open every morning in which state they remain through the day. Of late, cast iron beds have been introduced in place of wooden ones. The upper body clothing in use in summer both for boys and girls is entirely of cotton which, as they have spare suits to change with, are washed once a fortnight. In winter the boys are dressed in woollen cloth and they, as well as the girls, have complete dress suits for Sundays. Their linens are changed once a week. For a few months in summer both boys and girls go without shoes and stockings."*

All this certainly did not amount to soft or cosseted living, but the fact that only nine of these "boarders" died between 1792 and 1795 attests to high standards of hygiene and relative comfort when compared with the general squalor of the day.

*hundreds or thousands of threads at the same time.*

*The massive growth in productivity brought about by the inventions of Arkwright and his contemporaries transformed the textile industry and brought great social change in its wake. The days of the skilled, self-employed spinner, working at home during the hours of his or her choosing, were numbered. Capital-intensive industry brought about the development of the Factory System in which a large and disciplined workforce carried out closely controlled tasks throughout a standard working day within the confines of large mill buildings. This pattern of work has become familiar to us but was quite novel to the inhabitants of eighteenth century Scotland.*

*While discipline and tight control of standards was essential to the success of a spinning mill, great craft skill was not. Employers could therefore seek a less costly workforce, hence the predominance of children in the early textile industry.*

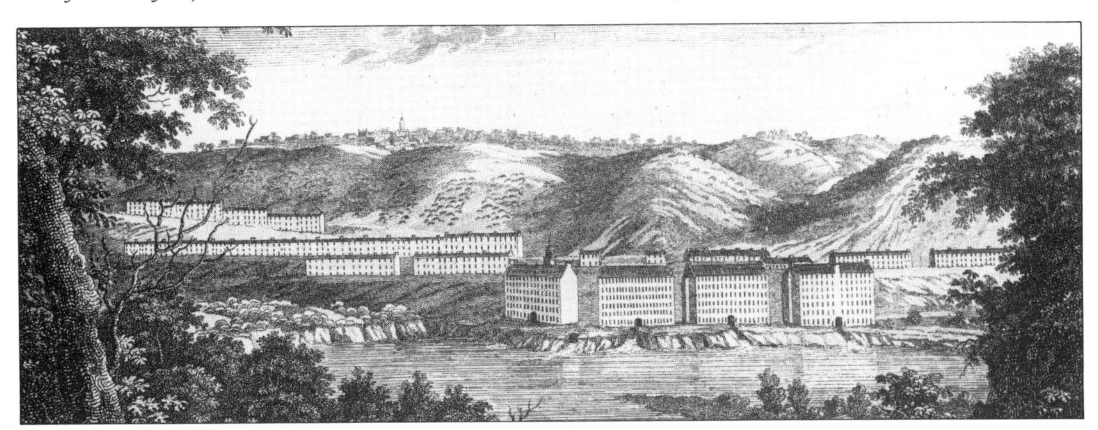

*The earliest illustrations of New Lanark are those of Robert Scott who visited the village in 1799. They show how little the place has changed since Dale's time. Braxfield, Long and Double Rows – at the entrance to the village – had been completed, as had Caithness Row, Dale's own home and the neighbouring manager's house and, most importantly, the four great mills, though not the store rooms which now hide the location of the water-wheels.*

*No. 1 mill, burnt out in October, 1788, was rebuilt the following year on five storeys (above), taken down (after 1945) to three storeys.*
*No. 2 mill, completed in 1788, was the same size as No. 1. It remained unchanged until the late nineteenth century when the Gourock Ropework Company widened the building and rebuilt the facade in somewhat ugly brickwork. No. 3 mill, completed by 1793, was destroyed by fire in 1819 and rebuilt by Robert Owen. No. 4 mill, also completed by 1793 and the largest of the earlier buildings, remained in use as a storehouse and dormitory until the second decade of Owen's management. It was destroyed by fire in 1883 and never replaced.*

## THE HIGHLAND IMMIGRATION

Another source of workers for the village were the Highlands. In 1793 it was noted that "a great proportion of the inhabitants are Highlanders, mostly from Caithness, Inverness and Argyleshire. Few of those from the West understand English". The first of these migrants were a group of 400 people from Skye whose ship, bound for Maryland, was forced by storms into Greenock in 1791. Dale offered them immediate employment in New Lanark, which over 100 took up. The following year he offered to provide accommodation for 200 Highland families as an encouragement to settle in the village rather than emigrate to North America.

Again the emphasis was on the importance of children for the workforce. Accommodation was made available on condition that families had three children fit for work who would be contracted for a period of four years in the mill. Children signified wealth in New Lanark. As one observer put it: "In other manufactures a woman who has a family and becomes a widow is generally in a most helpless situation. Here the case is very different, for the greater number of children a woman has she lives so much more comfortably and upon such account alone she is often a tempting object for a second husband."

The working day at New Lanark began at 6 in the morning and did not finish until 7 that evening after which the children were expected to attend school for two further hours. The only breaks were half an hour for breakfast and an hour for dinner. The food provided was excellent by the standards of the day. Breakfast consisted of as much porridge as the spinners could eat, while for dinner they were given barley broth with "good fresh beef", cheese or, in season, herrings and potatoes.

The school established by Dale at New Lanark provided an education not only for children working in the mill but also for the younger ones who attended during the day. By 1796 it employed 16 teachers who instructed 507 pupils in reading ("we heard some little boys read in a very superior manner" commented one visitor), writing and arithmetic. In addition, two part-time teachers taught sewing and church music. The main school had eight classes, each of which was provided with a "scheme of work . . . which so soon as they have accomplished, the scholars are transferred to the next higher class, and the teacher receives a small premium for everyone so qualified." Here, as Dale's biographer, David McLaren, has noted, was a structured and progressive system of basic education. In addition, the day school for the under-sixes was probably the first of its kind in any factory community: a noteworthy predecessor of Robert Owen's "rational system of infant education."

The dormitories of No. 4 mill provided accommodation for a fair proportion of the village but it was obviously necessary to put up more housing. The earliest houses appear to have been built near No. 1 mill. Then when Highland migrants began to arrive, the elegantly curved Caithness Row was built to house them. The rather starker streets at the other end of the village – Long Row, Double Row and Braxfield Row – were also erected in the 1790s and can be seen in the earliest known illustration of the village, dated 1799. The employment of workers living outside the village must have eased housing needs somewhat. Each morning they would have poured down the steep road into New Lanark following the same route taken in 1798 by Robert Owen. "Little did I imagine," he recalled in later years, "when I first saw this establishment, that I should ever become part proprietor and ultimately sole manager of it."

*Robert Owen's inspection of New Lanark with his future partners, Atkinson and Barton, in July 1799, is recorded in David Dale's Visitors Book (below right), as are Owen's two earlier visits. This book, perhaps more than any other surviving document, demonstrates the breadth of public interest in New Lanark, years before Owen had even set eyes on the village. The enormous variety of visitors included the pillars of the Scottish Establishment – the Lord Advocate, Dundases of Arniston, Hyndfords and Campbells of Jura, men of Enlightened Edinburgh like Henry Brougham and Henry Cockburn – soldiers and academics. Messrs. Melville, McCulloch and Walker, Students at St Andrews, Fellows from Kings College and Clare Hall, Cambridge – manufacturers, wrights, cabinetmakers, and, last but not least, foreign travellers – Mr Peschier from Geneva, Mr Rosentreter from Leipzig, Dr Morelli from Siena, Mr Matta from Lisbon (three times), Mr Jacobi from Düsseldorf, Mr Willink from Amsterdam, Mr Speed from Kentucky, Mr Gardiner from Savannah, Mr Aspinall from New York. Over 3000 people viewed David Dale's enterprise at New Lanark in the last five years of his ownership.*

| | | |
|---|---|---|
| July | 22 | John Mann |
| | " | Lieut. Campbell 51 Reg. |
| " | " | Mr Atkison Manchester |
| " | " | Mr J Barton Do |
| " | " | Mr Owen Do |
| " | 23 | Christian Fletcher from Bridge of Teat |
| " | " | Revd Thomas Brown Dalkeith |
| " | 27 | Robert Wight Kinghorn |
| " | " | Wm Wight Edinburgh |
| " | | [illegible] Blackwood Glasgow |
| | | Andw Peterson [illegible] |

# DAVID DALE (1739 – 1806)

"Men of strong, untrained energy . . . their success in life, however, was not wholly due to character and abilities. The lines had fallen to them in wondrous places. They were pioneer workers in the richest mine ever opened to human enterprise."

Robert Dale Owen's description rings true of Richard Arkwright (1732–1792), barber and wigmaker turned inventor and cotton-spinning magnate, but to have also applied it to his grandfather, David Dale, seems a trifle unfair. There can be no doubt that Dale, the son of a poor grocer from Stewarton in Ayrshire, seized the opportunities presented by the development of the Scottish cotton industry and died a rich man, but his concern for general economic development in Scotland, philanthropy, education and evangelical religion, suggests a man of wider vision – someone likely to have made his mark in any age.

Dale arrived in Glasgow at the age of 24 from an apprenticeship as a weaver in Paisley. In 1763 he took a one-room shop in Hopkirk's Land, near Glasgow Cross, where he set up as a textile merchant in partnership with Archibald Paterson, a friend and well-known candlemaker. This was a lucrative market to enter, and 20 years of ensuing prosperity culminated in Dale's appointment as first Glasgow agent for the Royal Bank. He acquired both a well-connected wife, Ann Caroline Campbell, and a mansion house in Charlotte Street, on what was then the south-east fringe of the city, designed for him by the best-known architect of the day, Robert Adam.

The Royal Bank appointment was the crowning achievement, confirming Dale as a member of the Glasgow – and, indeed, Scottish – financial establishment. The bank premises were in the old shop in Hopkirk's Land and, in time, it became one of the bank's most prosperous branches.

Now, however, Dale's interest shifted from trading to manufacturing. In the space of three years he set up a Turkey-red dyeworks at Dalmarnock (in partnership with George Macintosh, father of the inventor of the Macintosh raincoat), and cotton-mills at New Lanark, Catrine in Ayrshire, and Blantyre in Lanarkshire. In the 1760s Dale, in protest at the system of ecclesiastical patronage, had left the Church of Scotland and become a founder member of the strongly missionary Old Scotch Independent Church. As such, he would no doubt have appreciated the fact that seven years after his death, Blantyre was to be the birthplace of David Livingstone and that Scotland's greatest missionary found his first employment among the spinning jennies of the mill which Dale had established.

If New Lanark, Catrine and Blantyre were natural locations in which a Glasgow entrepreneur might want to establish mills, Dale's other choices of site point to a rather broader economic view. His concern at emigration from Scotland, apparent in his journey to Greenock to secure the services of Highland migrants for New Lanark, also expressed itself in the establishment of cotton mills in places as far apart as Oban, Stanley in Perthshire and Spinningdale in Sutherland. Spinningdale – the most conspicuously philanthropic of the ventures – was established in 1791 at the instigation of a local landowner, the fiercely independent former M.P., George Dempster of Dunnichen, with a specific intention to create industry, wealth and employment in the Highlands. Other aspects of Dale's philanthropy are to be seen in his schools – at Blantyre as well as New Lanark – and his role as director and benefactor of the Town's Hospital of Glasgow and the city's Royal Infirmary.

In 1800 Dale purchased the estate of Rosebank, near Cambuslang. This was clearly with a view to retirement, for he had by now begun the process of selling his mills. Robert Owen was the first beneficiary. Catrine followed New Lanark in 1801. Spinningdale was sold in 1804 and Dalmarnock in 1805. On 17th March, 1806, David Dale died at Rosebank.

*"Withal he was a genial, humourous man. He was given to hospitality and he would sing an old Scotch song with such feeling as to bring tears to the eyes."*

*David Dale's now demolished mill at Catrine, Ayrshire. Note its similarity to the original form of No. 1 mill at New Lanark, as shown in John Winning's painting (p. 15).*

# ROBERT OWEN (1771–1858)

Robert Owen, the Socialist. This is how he is described in library catalogues, but the reality is far more complicated. There is also Robert Owen the ambitious and at times none too scrupulous entrepreneur, the enlightened if despotic capitalist, the Utopian planner, the pioneer of the co-operative movement and trade unionism, the rejector of organised religion who in his last years became an ardent spiritualist.

Followers of the innovations at New Lanark have always been plentiful, but few could swallow Owen's complex and idiosyncratic philosophy whole.

"Who is your disciple? How many men possessed of your views, who will remain after you, are going to put them in practice" asked the American poet, Ralph Waldo Emerson, of the aged Owen.

"Not one," replied Owen.

This many-sided character was born in 1771 at Newtown, Montgomeryshire, Wales. His early career parallels that of his father-in-law: humble origins, local schooling (where Owen excelled, being taken on at the age of seven as the school "usher", or pupil-teacher, teaching the younger boys), early experience in the textile trade – Owen worked for haberdashers, first in Stamford, then in London – followed by a move from trade into manufacturing. Owen, however, became involved in manufacturing at a much younger age than David Dale. At the age of 19, he was engaged as superintendent of a large spinning mill in Manchester, the property of a Mr Drinkwater.

The young Owen had found himself at the thriving centre of cotton manufacturing and in the following few years he cultivated his contacts in the textile world as well as his management and manufacturing skills – he was the first to use the fine, long-fibred American sea-island cotton. His widening contacts eventually led him to Glasgow, to Caroline Dale and to partnership in New Lanark.

The description of the following 20 years, published by Owen in his *Life* is one of ordered progression: Owen's bold economic and social experiment, gradually brought to fruition in New Lanark and then promoted in the outside world with the village as a model. The reality seems to have been rather less tidy: the half-dozen years after 1812 witnessed Owen bringing together a sympathetic partnership for New Lanark and establishing his far-reaching reforms in the village – particularly in the field of education – while simultaneously producing his first major publication, *A New View of Society, or Essays on the Principle of the Formation of the Human Character.* He went throughout Britain and Western Europe, lobbying Parliament, the Church and anyone of influence (from Royalty to the leading economists of the day) on the importance of his general ideas, and specifically agitating for improvements in factory conditions.

The publication of Owen's *Report to the County of Lanark* in 1820 marked a turning point in his life. Despite its title and unlike *A New View of Society*, the *Report* was not concerned with the direct application of the lessons of New Lanark but was more of a general call for the transformation of society in which "the producer would have a fair and fixed proportion of all the wealth he creates." The context in which a transformation would take place were his proposed Villages of Co-operation "founded on the principle of united labour, expenditure and property, and equal privileges." The *Report to the County of Lanark* was a clear statement that New Lanark had become too small a stage for Robert Owen. America beckoned: New Harmony was to provide him with the opportunity to create his own "Village of Co-operation."

The New Harmony experiment was a disaster. When Owen finally returned to Britain in 1829 he had lost much of his personal fortune. In his absence, however, Owen's writings had made him the hero of the Co-operative Societies. Without his wealth Owen may have lost his influence in the corridors of power, but he was now accepted as a leader of the working class movement in a way that would have been well-nigh impossible for a rich mill owner.

In the following years, the busiest of his life, Owen provided the trade unions with a political philosophy of their own for the first time – it was, of course, very much his own, co-operative one – and he strived to organise them on a national basis. His efforts culminated in the formation of the Grand National Consolidated Trades Union in 1834. It was, however, an idea ahead of its time. The unionists had not yet gathered the strength to resist the repression by Government and employers which followed. The Union collapsed before the year was out. This marked the end of Owen as an influential force in public affairs.

Where, in all this, was the person who had brought Owen to New Lanark in the first place? Caroline Owen was left behind in the family home at Braxfield, just above New Lanark, to which the Owens had moved in 1808 from their house in the village. She saw little enough of her husband as he travelled through the country and abroad after 1813, and almost nothing at all of him during the American years. Her sons, too, travelled with their father to New Harmony.

"*Oh, my dear husband, how much I feel the want of you to advise with in a time of so much anxiety,*" she wrote plaintively at the time of their daughter Anne's illness in 1830. "*I hope you will remember next Thursday, the day when we became one – thirty-one years ago, and I think from what I feel myself, that we love one another as sincerely, and understand one another much better than we did thirty-one years ago.*"

By this time the loss of Owen's fortune had forced the sale of Braxfield and a move to a smaller house in Hamilton. Just one month after her mother's letter Anne Owen died, and the next spring Caroline Owen followed her.

Caroline remained David Dale's daughter to the last, a solid member of the Church in the face of both her husband's and her sons' dislike of organised religion. Robert Dale Owen tells a story of one of the most famous visitors to New Lanark – Crown Prince Nicolas of Russia – which illuminates the differing personalities of Caroline and Robert Owen. Nicolas stayed with the family and at dinner much was made of the Owens' silver, which bore a crest with a double-headed eagle similar to the Crown Prince's own. On the Russian's departure, Owen, in a typically impulsive manner, perhaps tinged with a hint of snobbery, sent the silver with him as a gift. It was a gesture which greatly irritated Caroline. If the Crown Prince had been either needy or a good friend, she could have sympathised, but this was a rich stranger and in a few days the gift would be forgotten. Robert Dale Owen heartily agreed with his mother. The blood of good-hearted, down-to-earth David Dale ran in his veins too.

*The houses built by Dale at New Lanark for his own family's use* **(above)** *and for the mill manager* **(below)**. *The mill manager's house was Robert and Caroline Owen's first home in the village.*

# THE GREAT EXPERIMENT

Robert Owen's arrival at New Lanark begins a remarkable story brightly embroidered with romance: the romance of his courtship with David Dale's eldest daughter Caroline, the romance of his first instinct that here was the place in which to turn his dreams for social reform into reality, all this against the romantic backdrop of the village itself in its leafy setting by the Falls of Clyde.

Owen's name is recorded for the first time in the Visitors Book at New Lanark in 1798. What had brought him there was a chance introduction to Caroline Dale in Glasgow. One senses that Caroline was attracted to the ambitious young Welshman from the start. Had Mr Owen, she asked, yet seen the beauties of the Falls of Clyde and her father's mills? If not, she could arrange introductions at New Lanark and would be most interested to hear his impressions of the place after the visit. They were to be strong ones. As he stood in front of New Lanark after an inspection of the mills, Owen declared: "Of all the places I have yet seen I should prefer this in which to try an experiment I have long contemplated and have wished to have an opportunity to put into practice."

He was to have his chance sooner than he could have expected. According to his own later account, two developments proceeded in tandem: the romance with Caroline blossomed and rumours grew that Dale was looking for a buyer for New Lanark. Although infatuated by him, Caroline would not marry without her father's consent and the young suitor had yet to meet, let alone gain the approval of David Dale, who by now was one of the wealthiest and best known businessmen in Glasgow. The idea occurred to Owen that an enquiry regarding the possible purchase of New Lanark would provide the necessary pretext for a meeting. Once again the Visitors Book tells the story: another visit to the village by Owen himself followed by a further trip in the company of two prospective partners, John Barton of Manchester and John Atkinson of London, both well established in the business world. Dale's initial scepticism as to the seriousness of the young-looking 27-year-old Owen was overcome – and New Lanark sold for £60,000. The Dale daughters remained that summer in the house that David Dale had built for the family in the centre of the village, and this provided Owen and Caroline with the opportunity to continue their courting on frequent walks along the Clyde. Dale himself, however, was hostile to the match. In the absence of a son he considered his eldest daughter was the appropriate person to continue his work. His preference for a husband for her was "an honest Scotchman."

On the other hand, Owen was now moving in the same social circles as Dale and winning friends there. Robert Scott Moncrieff, Dale's fellow agent of the Royal Bank of Scotland, and his wife were particularly taken by the Welshman and gradually wore down Dale's reluctance. Caroline Dale and Robert Owen were married in Dale's Glasgow home on 30th September, 1799. On the first day of the first year of the new century Robert Owen assumed the management of New Lanark. He had become both Dale's son-in-law and heir to the old man's greatest enterprise.

By contrast, the general mood in New Lanark that January was one of sadness and trepidation rather than excitement. The inhabitants of the village could not possibly have guessed how much their lives were to change for the better over the next 25 years. What they saw was their benevolent proprietor, respected Church leader and Glasgow magistrate, supplanted by a partnership based in Manchester and managed by a high-flying young man whom they must have suspected owed his position at least in part to nepotism. Even after seven years of the new management, a visitor would note that "*Mr Owen is said to be a very strict man and is not popular in the neighbourhood.*"

The problem was that even if, as Owen recalled in his autobiography, he had intended from the outset to embark on a long-contemplated experiment – and we have only his word for it that this reforming zeal was present from the begin-

*No. 3 mill, the only mill building erected by Robert Owen at New Lanark, replaced the original Dale building which was destroyed by fire in 1819.*

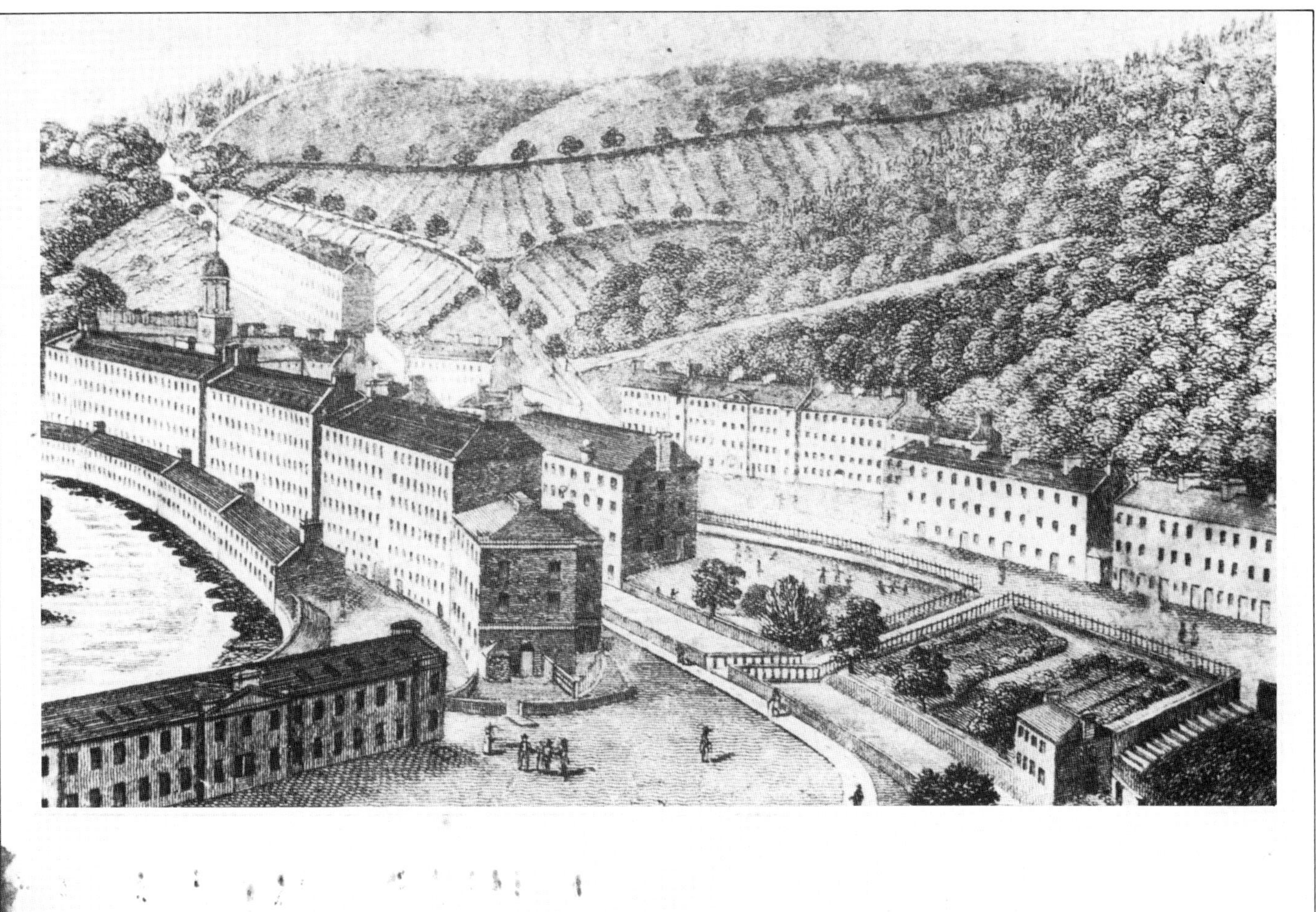

The Russians called the cotton they imported from New Lanark 'Picture-Yarn' because pictures of New Lanark, commissioned by Robert Owen from John Winning, decorated the labels on each bundle of cotton shipped from the village. An early example of successful commercial sponsorship of the arts!

ning rather than something that developed as a result of observing Dale's achievements – he also had the purely commercial interests of his partners to consider. Certainly the changes which occurred during the early years were geared very much towards economic rather than philanthropic ends. Hours of work were increased from 13 to 14 per day, individual output was monitored and watchmen were employed to patrol the streets and control any disorderly behaviour, particularly resulting from drunkenness. A worker found drunk on three occasions was subject to dismissal. The result, noted one observer, was that the workers were said "to be under better discipline and to do more work with fewer hands than in Mr Dale's time." In Owen's words, the early years were a time when he was "continually occupied in training the people, improving the village and machinery and in laying the foundations for future progress."

Only in 1806 did Owen begin to detect a softening in the attitude of the inhabitants towards him. It was during that year that an American embargo on the export of cotton forced up prices of the raw material to a point where spinning became uneconomic. The machines stopped and an unaccustomed silence fell over New Lanark for a few months. Throughout this period, however, Owen continued to pay the workforce full wages, not a single penny being deducted. It was in fact no more than Dale had done after No. 1 mill had burned down in 1788 – and it made good business sense, for recruiting a trained workforce in rural Lanarkshire after such a stoppage would have been well-nigh impossible. Nevertheless, according to Owen, his action made a favourable impression and at last he won a reasonable respect from the population of the village.

Robert Owen's fertile mind was now overflowing with ideas that would bring about a better organised and more benevolent system of management in New Lanark, but it was inevitable that he would eventually feel fettered by the constraints of partners with purely commercial interests. Significantly, the storm broke over his plans to build a school – for which ground had been cleared in 1809. While Owen's management of New Lanark and the profits being drawn from the mills might have been quite acceptable to his partners, they could not see the financial benefits of lavish expenditure on an educational institute. The partnership with Atkinson and Barton was dissolved in 1810 and Owen found new partners among the Glasgow business circles to which his marriage had introduced him. They included several relations of Caroline Campbell, his wife's mother, but proved equally unsatisfactory. The new men were no more interested in Owen's rapidly developing

**Opposite:** *Two watercolours of New Lanark by John Winning c. 1818. Winning taught painting at Owen's Institution, where his daughter, Janet, was also employed as a teacher. Four of the Winning children, including Janet, emigrated to the United States. Several of their letters home have survived and provide a fascinating insight into migrant life as well as testifying to the high standards of literacy provided by a New Lanark education. John Winning died in 1839. Of his children who did not emigrate, three were still living in New Buildings as late as 1881.*

theories than his old partners and also became increasingly concerned – with, it would appear, good reason – over Owen's management of his personal finances. In 1813 the second partnership was dissolved and Owen found himself forced to agree to the auctioning of New Lanark.

## PLOTS AND A ROUP

Owen resolved to establish a new partnership. He suspected that his ex-partners believed he could not raise the purchase price and were therefore denigrating what had become of the village under Owen's management in order to buy back New Lanark themselves at a bargain price. What followed was a fine example both of Owen's business acumen and his ability to put an increasing renown as a social reformer to good use. He travelled to London, ostensibly to supervise the publication of his latest essays but also secretly to negotiate a new partnership. He found six sympathetic individuals who, unlike the Glasgow "hard men", were as interested in investing in Owen's "great experiment" as in what were by now the largest cotton-spinning mills in the country. These were predominantly Quakers – men such as the wealthy John Walker of Arno's Grove in London and the successful business man William Allen – but also included the economist and later founder of London University, Jeremy Bentham. It was, Owen later boasted, the one sound investment that this reclusive academic ever made.

Meanwhile, back in Glasgow, the former partners had found a wealthy new investor prepared to take Owen's place, and had poached John Humphreys, Owen's under-manager, with promises of advancement. They were also convinced that New Lanark was about to become theirs at a knock-down price, and had laid on a sumptuous banquet to follow the auction.

On 31st December, 1813, the sale took place in Glasgow. Owen instructed his solicitor, Alexander Macgregor, to raise the bidding by no more than £100 at a time. (Three of Owen's prospective partners had secretly arrived in Glasgow.) His opponents, Owen noted, came into the saleroom with great confidence – they had not heard that Owen had found a single supporter. Bidding began at £60,000. Each time the Glasgow men offered another £1,000, Macgregor topped it by £100. By the time the price had reached £80,000 the old partners were becoming distinctly uneasy. They retired for consultation but on their return the same pattern continued, Macgregor adding another £100 each time they raised the price. The old partners took the bidding up to £110,000 – Macgregor offered £110,100. "Their agitation excessive, their lips blue", they retired again. As they returned one observer of Macgregor's bidding exclaimed excitedly: "The little one will get it!" Owen remained in the corner of the room seemingly impassive and inattentive. The price reached £114,000. Macgregor added another £100 and the property was knocked down to him. The old partners were crestfallen. They realised Owen had gained a bargain but having convinced themselves and their intended new partner that there would be no opposition, they had been unable to persuade him to continue bidding.

The triumphant Owen and his new partners then set out for New Lanark. As they approached the village they were greeted by a huge crowd which, removing the horses from their traces pulled Owen's open coach the last mile themselves. That evening the lights of every house in New Lanark were ablaze – except those of the wretched under-manager, John Humphreys. He and Owen's opponents were gathered glumly around the table at the celebratory banquet they had been unable to cancel. The wine and food brought out for what they had expected to be their great coup was the very best but, Owen heard, they sat in stony and miserable silence.

## OWENISM: FROM PRINCIPLES TO PRACTICE

New Year's Day, 1814, was in many ways a much more significant date in the history of New Lanark than the same day 14 years before when Owen had become Manager. Not only did he now have as free a hand as he was ever likely to have but his ideas were fully thought out. The first essay of his *New View of Society or the Formation of Character* had been published and the other three essays in the series completed. "Owenism" was born. It was time for him to put its first principles into action and "*commence in earnest the great experiment which was to prove to me by practice the truth or error of the principles which had been forced on my convictions as everlasting principles of truth . . . to commence the most important experiment for the happiness of the human race that had yet been instituted at any time in any part of the world.*"

These principles were relatively straightforward. Wondrous though the technical developments of the previous half century had been they had ignored the most important element for a successful Industrial Society: the welfare of the workforce. The character of people, Owen believed, was formed entirely by their surroundings. The exploitation of labour – particularly child labour – and the squalid conditions which he had witnessed on his travels around Britain, were bound to produce discontented and inefficient workers. Good housing, good education and disciplined, well organised but benevolent working conditions would produce a contented and efficient workforce. Philanthropy would go hand in hand with economic advantage. It was this creed that he was to preach by example to the thousands of people who visited New Lanark in the following decade and the tens of thousands more who read his numerous essays on the subject. "*All the houses in the village,*" he wrote, "*form parts of the establishment, all united and working together as one machine, proceeding day by day with the regularity of clockwork.*"

Commercial success at New Lanark, then, was the vital ingredient in providing credibility for Owen's principles. The system of management he now introduced was indeed remarkably advanced for the times. Mill operations were placed under the management of four superintendents appointed by Owen. Detailed records were kept of daily productivity and costs. Owen introduced his famous "silent monitor . . . a four-sided piece of wood about two inches long and one broad, each coloured – one side black,

(Repairs of Lamps, Tables, Stoves, &c.

Clothing for Children

| | | | | |
|---|---|---|---|---|
| Boys Dresses 138 at 5/4 | 36 16 " | | | |
| Girls Do 129 at 6/2 | 39 15 6 | | | |
| Tartan 81¼ Yards | 6 8 7 | | | |
| Wm Robertson | | | | |
| 24 Vocal Pieces (Print & Paper) 0 . 3 . 8 | | | | |
| Copy Lines . 1 . | | | | |
| Repairing 18 Flutes 1 . 4 . | | | | |
| Concert & Ball (Print & Paper) . 4 . 8 | | | | |
| an Index . 2 . 3 | | | | |
| 56 Cards of Education . 5 . 9 | | | | |
| Binding 5 Music Books . 5 . 10 | | | | |
| 13 Robertson's Ch. Music 4/ 2 . 12 . | | | | |
| Binding Do . 15 . 2 | | | | |
| 5 . 14 . 4 | | | | |
| less Discount . 7 . 4 | 5 7 . | | | |
| Luke O'Niel – Phrenological Head | . 12 6 | 5 19 6 | 47 | |
| Exhibition of a Crocodile | " 5 " | 12 2 1 | 54 5 | |
| James Earl Exhibiting Wild Beasts to the Children | 2 " " | | | |
| John Winning Painting | 18 8 8 | | | |
| C. D. Whitwell 6 mos. Salary Painting Subjects of Natural history &c. | 50 " " | | | |
| Gratuity | 50 " " | 201 9 5 | | |
| Mary Young " . 9/ | 2 " 6 | | | |
| Mary Martin 1½ . " 10/ | " 15 4 | | | |
| " " Night 2⅓ . . 2/6 | " 6 8 | | | |
| Janet Winning 1½ " . 9/ | " 16 6 | | | |
| " " Night 2⅓ " . 2/6 | " 6 8 | | | |
| David Budge 4½ " . 21/ | 4 14 6 | | | |
| ... King " . 18/ | 4 1 " | | | |

St Petersburgh 7/19 Septr 1815 We had this pleasure last post informing you
recd 13 Octr of the arrival of the Fame with your 82 Bales &
that if we could make the prices we expected it was our intention to profit by
the present uncommonly Brisk demand & high prices to realize these yarns
& the 40 or 50 Bales you are shipping via Leith which last it
was necessary to include not only to secure such prices
but because they could not be seperated from those ar-

another blue, the third yellow and the fourth white." This was suspended in a conspicuous position by the workplace of every employee, indicating to the superintendent the performance for the previous day: black for bad, blue for indifferent, yellow for good and white for excellent. Owen himself could walk through the mills and tell at a glance how each employee was shaping up. There was, he said, "no beating, no abusive language . . . I merely looked at the person and then at the colour . . . I could at once see by the expression of countenance what was the colour which was shown."

The same remarkably advanced approach to social and economic organisation was extended to every aspect of village life. A Sick Fund was established to which the mill workers contributed a 60th part of their wages, as was a Savings Bank which held deposits to the value of over £3000 by 1818. The village shop – probably erected in 1813 – was stocked by Owen, who sold at almost cost price goods he had bought wholesale. The inhabitants of New Lanark, he noted, "*had previously been necessitated to buy inferior articles, highly adulterated at enormous prices, making their purchases at the small grocery and grog shops, chiefly on credit, and the butcher's meat was generally little better than skin and bone. By the time the arrangements to provide for their wants and food, clothing, etc., were completed, some of the larger families were spending £2 per week, and my new arrangements to supply their wants saved them 10 shillings weekly. The grocery and grog shops speedily disappeared and the population soon relieved themselves from the debts contracted to them.*" Once again, benevolence went hand in hand with commercial expediency and disciplined organisation. Quality goods were made available at reasonable prices, enabling Owen to keep a check on the sale of such undesirables as whisky and so control drunkenness in the village.

## CRADLE OF INFANT EDUCATION

The needs of the young were an understandably important factor in a village with so many children. Owen wrote: "*The houses of the poor and working classes generally are altogether unfit for the training of young children . . . these considerations created in me the first thoughts respecting the necessity of infant education to be based on the true principle of forming character from the earliest period at which infants could leave their parents.*"

The single greatest legacy of Robert Owen's New Lanark is in the field of education and this is reflected in his principal monuments in the village: the School and the New Institution for the Formation of Character, later known as the Institute. It was within the walls of these buildings in remote Clydesdale that the system of infant education as we now know it in Britain – and indeed much of the world – began in 1816. By the end of that decade thousands of fascinated visitors had passed through Owen's schoolrooms and taken their impressions home to every part of Britain and beyond – to France and Germany, Switzerland and Austria, Russia and America.

Eighteenth century philosophers, including Jean-Jacques Rousseau, had suggested the idea of the open-minded adult character formed by an education that was affectionate, undogmatic and close to nature. It was, however, left to a self-made Welshman in a Lanarkshire village – no doubt influenced by his own childhood memories as pupil-teacher, the foundations of the school system laid by Dale and, possibly not least, the beauty of his surroundings – to put these theories into practice.

As early as 1809 Owen had cleared the land for a school building at New Lanark and, as we have seen, it was the ambitious nature of these plans that largely precipitated the crisis of his first partnership. It was to be seven frustrating years until the New Institution for the Formation of Character was opened, but they at least allowed Owen time to study the ideas of such contemporary British educational pioneers as Andrew Bell and Joseph Lancaster (whom he brought to Scotland in 1812) and to put together the most thorough plans for his "new rational infant school."

On 1st January, 1816, the Institution was declared open by Owen. Sixteen years to the day after he had assumed the management of New Lanark, he had achieved his greatest ambition. Characteristically, he did not miss the opportunity to enlarge upon his vision. The entire population of New Lanark was brought into the new building and given a long address, mercifully broken by a musical interlude. In summary, he told them: "*I know that society may be formed so as to exist without crime, without poverty, with health greatly improved, with little if any misery, and with intelligence and happiness increased a hundred-fold, and no obstacle whatsoever intervenes at this moment, except ignorance, to prevent such a state of society from becoming universal.*"

Owen's Institution, which was to play such an important part in his great experiment to prove the possibility of bringing about this state of

*"St Petersburgh 7/19 September 1815. We had this pleasure last post informing you of the arrival of the 'Fame' with your 82 Bales and that if we could make the prices we expected it was our intention to profit by the present uncommonly brisk demand and high prices to realize these yarns and the 40 or 50 Bales you are shipping via Leith. . ."*

*Copy letter to Owen from his Russian agent, Allan Stewart. Russia was one of New Lanark's largest markets for cotton yarn. Note the dual dating of the letter which was necessary before Russia adopted the Western calendar.*

**Opposite:** *Dancing Classes at New Lanark, with the animal mural as a backdrop.*
*The School* **(above)** *and the Institute* **(below)** *today.*
*An insight into the advanced methods of education in New Lanark can be gleaned from the entries in the school accounts book:*

| *Clothing for Children* | |
|---|---|
| *Boys Dresses* | |
| *138 at 5/4* | (£) 36 16 |
| *Girls Dresses* | |
| *129 at 6/2* | (£) 39 15 6 |
| *Tartan* | |
| *81¼ yards* | (£) 6 8 4 |

*Materials for the curious amalgamation of Highland and Roman Dress which Robert Owen felt would allow the school children proper freedom of movement were supplied by him.*
*Teaching aids including '24 Vocal Pieces (Print and Paper)', 'Repairing 18 Flutes', '56 Cards of Education', 'Binding 5 Music Books' and a 'Phrenological Head'. 'Exhibition of a Crocodile 5(s)' and*
*'James Earl Exhibiting Wild Beasts for the Children £2'*
*'John Winning Painting (£) 18.8.8*
*C V Whitwell 6 mo(nth)s Salary Painting Subjects of Natural History, etc.* (£) 50.0.0
*Gratuity* (£) 50.0.0'
*Winning taught painting in the*

*School but the murals of animals which hung there were the work of Miss Whitwell, a teacher who had come to New Lanark from London and was later involved in the Owenite Community of Orbiston near Motherwell established in 1825.*

*Teachers' wages included those of Mary Young who, with James Buchanan, played an important part in the establishment of the infant school, and David Budge, the dancing master. Also included are payments for teaching older pupils in the evening. It is interesting to note the importance accorded to Budge's role; at 21s a week his salary is the same as those of the best paid teachers of academic subjects. The salaries bill alone made the New Lanark School expensive to run, but educational costs in the village were offset against profits from the village shop.*

society, was described by his son, Robert Dale Owen. It was housed on two storeys:

"*The upper storey is divided into two apartments. One, which is the principal schoolroom fitted up with desks and forms on the Lancasterian plan, having a free passage down the centre of the room, is about 90 feet long, 40 feet broad and 20 feet high. It is surrounded, except at one end where a pulpit stands, with galleries which are convenient when this room is used, as it frequently is, either as a lecture room or a place of worship.*

"*The other apartment on the second floor is of the same width and height. The walls are hung round with the representations of the most striking zoological and mineralogical specimens including quadrupeds, birds, fishes, reptiles, insects, shells, minerals, etc. At one end there is a gallery adapted for the purpose of an orchestra and at the other are hung very large representations of the two hemispheres. This room is used as a lecture and ballroom and it is here that dancing and singing lessons are daily given. The lower storey is divided into three apartments. It is in these that the younger classes are taught reading.*"

In 1816 the School had 14 teachers and 274 pupils – a good teacher-pupil ratio even by modern standards. The hours of attendance were from 7.30 a.m. until 5 p.m., with two breaks in the summer, and 10 a.m. until 2 p.m. in winter. Children came into the school when they were just 18 months old and stayed until the age of ten or 12, when they went on to work in the mills. Here was another example of Owen's equation of benevolence with a thriving economy. He may have lost child labour, but in taking children into school at such an early age he could count on the mothers of even very young children being available for work. An American visitor noted in 1818: "This baby school is of great consequence to the establishment for it enables the mothers to shut up their houses in security and to attend to their duties in the factory without concern for their families."

The basis of Owen's education system was the encouragement of an appetite for knowledge not through punishments and rewards, both of which were banned from the School, but through nurturing the senses. Singing, dancing and the appreciation of nature were all to play a part in this process. As often as possible lessons took place out-of-doors, either in the large playground attached to the school or on walks around the village. When the weather did not permit this, the teachers were encouraged to bring natural objects – flowers, interesting stones, even animals – into the classrooms. This formed the starting point for lessons in nature study, geography and history: subjects taught even to the younger children for, in Robert Dale Owen's words, this was "almost the first knowledge which nature directs an infant to acquire."

The specific encouragement of dancing and singing particularly interested visitors to New Lanark.

"*These children,*" reminisced Owen, "*standing up 70 couples at a time in the dancing room and often surrounded with many visitors would, with the utmost elegance and natural grace, go through all the dances of Europe with so little direction from their Master that the strangers*

*would be unconscious that there was a Dancing Master in the room.*

*"In their singing lessons 150 would sing at the same time, their voices being trained to harmonise, and it was delightful to hear them singing the old popular Scotch songs, which were great favourites with most strangers from the unaffected simplicity and heart feelings with which these songs were sung by these children whose natures had been naturally and rationally cultivated."*

Each evening the Institute remained open for older children – ten to 20-year-olds who were working in the mills by day – to attend classes, and it is clear that Owen wanted to develop the building not just for adult education but also for general community use. By 1818 there were plans for public kitchens and eating rooms in the Institution, and it was almost certain these developments led to the erection of another building a few yards away to serve the educational needs of the younger children. The School was completed by 1819, and the classes appear to have moved in by 1822. It was here that New Lanark's children continued to be educated well into the 1880s.

Owen had no particular desire to see the younger children taught religion or be "annoyed" by books. However, under parental pressure he gave way on both matters. If he had not done so there would undoubtedly have been further pressure from his predominantly Quaker partners. As it was, the partners – particularly William Allen who, of all of them, took the greatest interest in New Lanark – remained concerned about Owen's educational methods. Physical education at New Lanark encompassed not just singing and dancing but also "military exercises". These activities, particularly when performed under the eyes of numerous fascinated and susceptible visitors were hardly likely to meet with Quaker approval. The partners, Allen had to tell Owen, were determined "to prevent him from making New Lanark an infidel establishment". Finally in January, 1824, the outnumbered Owen was brought to account. The most treasured aspect of his "great experiment" was considerably diluted: dancing, singing and music were no longer to be provided by the Company, and even the dress stipulated and provided by Owen for the children – a cross between a Roman tunic and a kilt, which he considered would provide freedom of movement and so freedom of spirit – was, in the interests of "decency", to go.

The essential foundations of New Lanark remained unchanged, but it is easy to appreciate Owen's frustrations, fettered once again as he was by a partnership – this time one for which he had fought so hard. Now, moreover, his appetite was whetted by extensive travel and the increasing influence of his ideas both at home and abroad. When Richard Flower arrived at New Lanark in the summer of 1824 to enquire whether Owen would be interested in buying into the experimental co-operative venture at Harmony in Indiana, Owen was altogether susceptible to the offer.

"New Lanark or Harmony?" he asked his son.

"Harmony," answered Robert Dale Owen without hesitation – and in doing so answered for his father too.

In December, 1824, the two Robert Owens sailed for America. The Owen era at New Lanark was at an end and the years at New Harmony were about to begin.

*The rhymes which James Buchanan taught the children of New Lanark epitomise his gentle art of communication:*

*The Cow*

*Come, children listen to me now,*
*And you shall hear about the cow,*
*You'll find her useful, live or dead,*
*Whether she's black, or white, or red.*
*When milkmaids milk her morn or night,*
*She gives us milk so fresh and white,*
*And this we little children think,*
*Is very nice for us to drink.*
*The milk we skim and shake in churns,*
*And then it soon to butter turns.*
*The curdled milk we press and squeeze,*
*And so we make it into cheese.*
*The skin, with lime and bark together,*
*The tanner tans and makes it leather,*
*And without this what should we do*
*For soles for every boot and shoe?*
*This is not all, as you will see:*
*Her flesh is food for you and me;*
*Her feet provide us glue and oil;*
*Her bones tend to improve the soil;*
*And last of all, if ta'en with care,*
*Her horns make combs to comb our hair.*
*And so we learn, thanks to our teachers,*
*That cows are very useful creatures.*

*The Sheep*

*"Hark now to me and silence keep,*
*And you will hear about the sheep;*
*For sheep are useful, and you know*
*That on their backs the wool does grow.*
*The sheep are taken once a year,*
*And plunged in water cool and clear;*
*And there they swim and never bite*
*While men do wash them clean and white."*

*"In June, 1814 I went to (New) Lanark, being then thirty years. In November, 1815, I commenced my new era, and gave up the desire of becoming rich or great, content if my life would be useful." These were the sentiments of James Buchanan, an East Lothian weaver, who became the first teacher in Robert Owen's infant school. His unaffected, untutored simplicity, his gentle ability to kindle the imaginations of his charges, made Buchanan the ideal man to fulfil Owen's educational principles. He would, recalled his grand-daughter, march the children "round the room to the strains of his flute. Then he marched them through the village, and allowed them to amuse themselves on the banks of the Clyde, and march back again. . . . He never grew up, but was always simple-hearted and natural as a child, and had a child's power to imagine and dramatise."*

*So impressed were some of New Lanark's more distinguished visitors that they persuaded Owen to release Buchanan to set up a school in London where, in 1819, he was established as Teacher to the Westminster Free Day Infant Asylum.*

*In 1839 Buchanan decided to emigrate to New Zealand to establish infant schools there. He never got further than Cape Town, where his son persuaded him to stay, and where he lived until his death in 1857.*

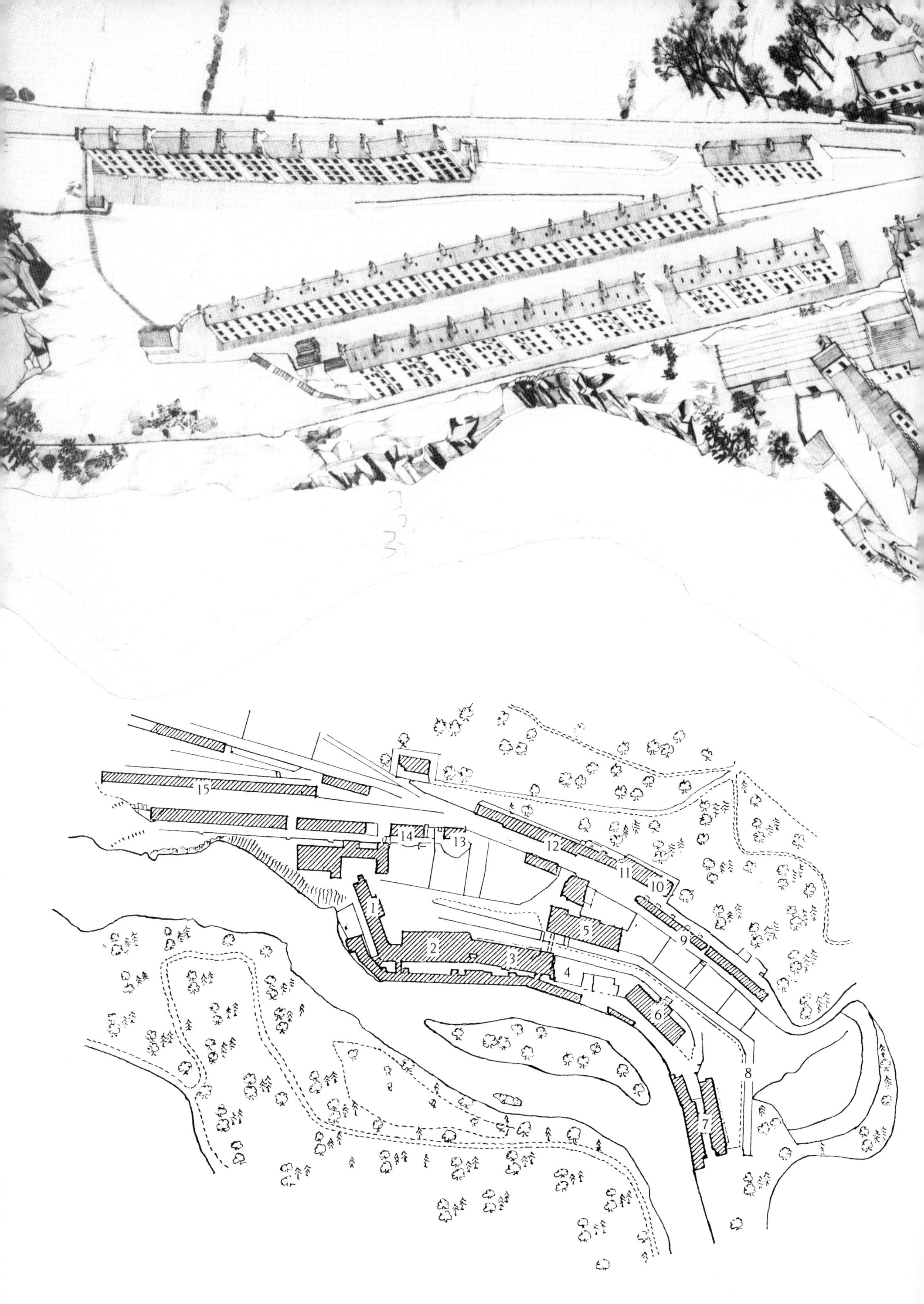
15
14
13
12
11
10
1
2
3
5
9
4
6
8
7

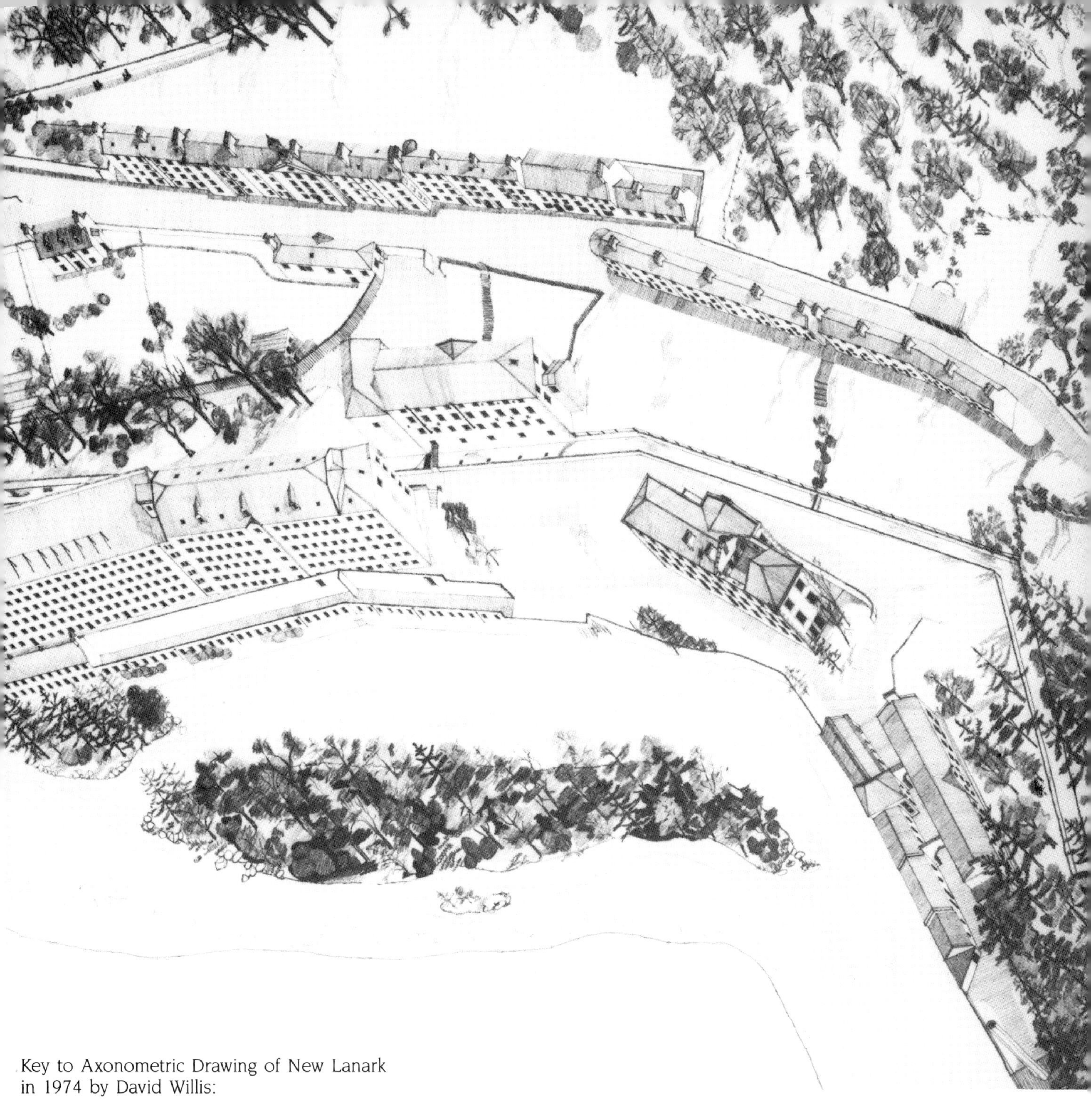

Key to Axonometric Drawing of New Lanark in 1974 by David Willis:

1 No. 1 mill
2 No. 2 mill
3 No. 3 mill
4 Site of No. 4 mill
5 The Institute
6 The School (with collapsed roof)
7 Workshops and Dyeworks
8 Mill Lade
9 Caithness Row and Counting House
10 Village Store
11 Nursery Buildings
12 New Buildings
13 Robert Owen's House
14 David Dale's House
15 The Rows

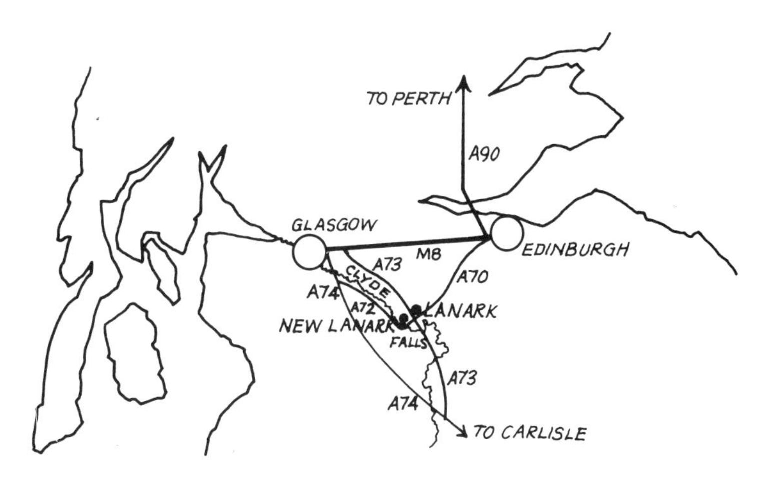

It was George Rapp, a farmer from Wurtemburg driven to America by religious intolerance, who founded the first community at Harmony, Indiana, in 1814. In 1824 he decided to move his colonists to another site (lest, it was said, they became too prosperous and comfortable and forgot their faith) and dispatched Richard Flower, an Englishman who had helped found a colony in neighbouring Illinois, to enquire whether Robert Owen might be interested in purchasing the existing settlement. Owen arrived in December, 1824, purchased the settlement in the following April and renamed it New Harmony. His aim was the creation of a Village of Co-operation of the type first advocated in the "Report to the County of Lanark".

The enterprise seemed doomed from the start. The settlers who arrived by the hundred appeared, to Robert Dale Owen, to be a "heterogeneous collection of radicals, enthusiastic devotees to principle, honest latitudinarians and lazy theorists, with a sprinkling of unprincipled sharpers thrown in". The principles of the village's management were as curious and contradictory a rag-bag as its inhabitants. Equality was the order of the day but Owen, as founder and sole proprietor, proposed to appoint the committee of management himself. Anyone was welcome to settle in the village, but anyone did not include "persons of colour" who were specifically barred.

Soon the farmers who sustained the community were complaining that they received no more reward than the settlement's hangers-on. At dances, where partners were assigned by the drawing of lots "the young ladies turned up their noses at the democratic dancers who in this way often fell to their lot". The government of New Harmony had disintegrated into a series of squabbling factions by the time that Robert Owen left the settlement in June, 1828.

There is a poignant footnote to the story of New Harmony. While Owen was squandering his fortune on the ill-fated community, George Rapp had led his followers to a new settlement in Pennsylvania which with cruel, if guileless, irony he named Economy. It prospered greatly throughout the nineteenth century.

In one important, though quite unplanned, respect Robert Owen did bequeath America a fine legacy. All four of his sons had followed him to New Harmony and subsequently settled in America, becoming United States citizens. William Owen settled quietly at New Harmony, but the other three were each to play an important role in the development of their adopted country. Richard Owen became Professor of Natural Sciences at Nashville University. David Dale Owen, appointed United States Geologist in 1839, carried out pioneering surveys of what were then the north west frontier territories of the country. Robert Dale Owen became a member of the United States Congress in 1843, where he was instrumental in pushing through legislation for women's rights and for state provided education. The achievement for which he was to be best remembered, however, was his central role in the establishment of the Smithsonian Institution. It was Robert Dale Owen who introduced the Bill in Congress for founding the Smithsonian Institution and it was he and his brother, David, who are said to have drawn up the initial plans for the Smithsonian building.

# THE FORGOTTEN YEARS

*Braxfield House (above), to which the Owens moved in 1808, probably became the home of Charles and Henry Walker when Caroline Owen moved to Hamilton in 1828. It was from here that the Walkers managed New Lanark for over 50 years. Charles (born 1798) and Henry (born 1807) were the sons of John Walker (1767–1824), Owen's principal partner after 1813, and his wife Sarah. Even before his father's death Charles was involved in the affairs of New Lanark. He and William Allen were among the partners who visited New Lanark in early 1824 and he remained actively involved in the affairs of the village into his eighties.*

Robert Owen severed his remaining links with New Lanark in 1825. During the century and a half which followed, the village, hidden in its vale, was largely forgotten by the outside world. Subsequent proprietors did not possess Owen's flair for self-promotion or Dale's extensive connections within the Scottish Establishment. Only the inhabitants remained aware that many of the Founding Fathers' principles continued to be practised in the village. In the spring of 1903 Frank Podmore, Owen's biographer, visited New Lanark for the first time:

"*My guide, John Campbell Melrose, told me that in his boyhood some 30 years back, he and the other children still danced every morning from 7.15 to 8 a.m. The dancing room was one of the upper rooms in the old building and the name of the last dancing master was David Dunn. According to my guide the paintings and maps were only taken down when the School gave place to a Board School. A number of large cardboard plates of flowers and plants were still to be seen at the time of my visit; a few geometrical models and other things; and especially four of the original linen rolls which used to be hung on the walls, wound on rollers like a map. They were 3 or 4 feet wide and the largest was perhaps 40 feet in length. Two of these rolls were filled with musical notation and tunes. The other two were covered with pictures, painted in oils, illustrating various members of the animal kingdom. There were zoophytes, worms, shells, crustacea, insects of the several orders, batrachia, reptiles and at the torn end of one roll, a tiger rampant in his jungle.*"

This evidence of continuity in the affairs of New Lanark is not surprising. Charles and Henry Walker who managed the village for over 50 years after Owen's departure were the sons of John Walker, Owen's wealthy and much respected partner, and whatever differences the Quakers may have had with Owen, their overall objectives were not so dissimilar. Even when this thread was broken with the sale of New Lanark by the Walkers in 1881, change was not drastic – for the purchaser, Henry Birkmyre of the Gourock Ropework Company, and his descendants, appreciated and respected the principles that made the village so special.

## TENTMAKERS TO BERTRAM MILLS

What the Birkmyres did do, however, was diversify production. The weaving of New Lanark-spun cotton, hitherto largely a cottage industry in the village, now became an important part of the mill's output. The weavers produced everything from deckchair covers and military canvas to the tenting material for the Big Top of Bertram Mills' Circus. Villagers can still remember getting concessionary tickets when the circus came to town. Rope and fishing-nets were the mainstay of the Gourock company and these too were now manufactured in New Lanark.

New product lines required skills not available locally. Manxmen came to pass on their abilities in net-making, while the greater involvement in weaving brought more Irish families to add to the number who had already settled in the village by the mid nineteenth century. A Works Manager's Report of the 1880s contains a reminder to clamp down on the over-enthusiastic celebration of St Patrick's Day in the village, but for the most part assimilation into the life of the community seems to have been relatively painless. The majority of the incomers were Scotch-Irish, sharing the same culture, religion and names as the locals, and this probably made integration that much easier.

Despite diversification, cotton-spinning remained King in New Lanark. The great water-wheels continued to turn, right through the nineteenth century and, in the case of the Dye Works at least, were not replaced by water turbines until as late as 1929. Auxiliary steam power was introduced by the 1880s but the mills were still subject to the vagaries of the seasons. In winter the wheel-houses were heated to prevent the water-wheels freezing, but nothing could stop the build-up of ice in the mill lade. Summer, too, presented problems as the water level fell and the turn of the wheels became even more sluggish.

## HEAT AND DUST

Raw cotton – the lifeblood of New Lanark – continued to be landed, as it had been in Owen's days, at Liverpool. Most of it was grown in America, though the produce of other countries also came under the scrutiny of the experienced mill hands. The fine, long-fibred Egyptian cotton was remembered with affection, while the Indian variety was particularly disliked. The cotton bales were brought by rail to Lanark and from there to New Lanark, initially by horse and cart, later by a bulky steam-powered traction-engine which once caused great excitement when, taking the hairpin bend into the village too sharply, it wedged itself firmly across the entrance road. It was eventually replaced by a more orthodox lorry and finally, in the last years of the mill's

DANGER
NO ENTRY
VILLAGE STORE

operation, the procedure was changed completely: contractors brought the bales directly from the docks by road.

The cleaning and preparation of cotton for spinning took place on the lower floors of the mill buildings. It was a notoriously dirty business and clerical staff, hurrying through these rooms, marvelled at the resilience of those who spent their working days in this dust-laden atmosphere. They were assured by doctors that vegetable dust was infinitely less harmful than the mineral variety which caused such problems in the nearby mines, but at least one worker recalls that he and three others resigned over conditions in the carding room.

The spinning rooms, although cleaner, could also be uncomfortable places to work in. Cotton "ran" in conditions of high humidity and these were provided by steam heating carried in great pipes which ran through the rooms just below ceiling level. A moist 80 degrees Fahrenheit prevailed and workers can still remember the shock of emerging from this tropical environment into a cold winter's night. They would have been working a ten-hour day from the time that the bell on New Buildings summoned them at 6 a.m. – later, work began at 8 a.m. – until 5.30 p.m., with mealbreaks at 9 and 12.15. On Saturdays, too, they found themselves at work – though only for the morning. It was an even longer day for the numerous mill hands who came not from the village itself but from settlements as far afield as Wishaw and Douglas, Carluke and Forth and who, before the advent of public transport in 1945, had to walk down from Lanark each morning. Only in the last few years of the mill's operation did the Company lay on buses for these workers.

*In the humid heat of the spinning rooms, the mill workers often went barefoot.*

COMMUNITY AND COMPANY

Hard conditions indeed, but the mill workers seem to have been generally satisfied with their lot. Within the mills there was a spirit of cooperation, particularly prior to the introduction of piece-work between the World Wars. Labour relations were good. The only recorded strike in the whole history of New Lanark, which took place during the Second War, was a desultory affair of just a few days. The harmony which prevailed was undoubtedly the result in part of the closeness of a community living and working in a self-contained world. Managers and mill hands spent their leisure hours together, playing badminton in the Hall, as the Institute had come to be known, or sharing newspapers, books and games of dominoes in the reading room. The spirit of Dale and Owen was not forgotten either, though managers inevitably regarded Owen's work as that of a benevolent capitalist rather than of the "notorious Socialist" he had come to be branded by less sympathetic industrialists. As in Owen's day, workers were not paid particularly well compared with spinners elsewhere – around 10 shillings a week for trainees rising to about 35 shillings a week in the 1930s for fully trained men – but they were more than adequately compensated through low rents (2 shillings a week was normal for a New Lanark house of the time), free electric light from the water turbine installed in 1898, and the facilities of the Hall and village shop. The Company still managed the shop on a cooperative basis which provided villagers with a regular dividend on profits.

*Typical accommodation in the village.*

Apart from the electric lighting, Robert Owen would probably not have noticed a great deal of change in the village homes if he had returned a century after his departure from New Lanark. Living areas were small – it was quite common to find families of ten and 12 in two rooms – and internal services few. Heat and fuel for cooking was provided by coal kept in bunkers at the entrance to each tenement and burned in ranges. Pails were an important element of household life: each home had its white enamel bucket for bringing water in from the village pumps and a galvanised one for removing "slops" which would be poured down drains in the street. Public lavatory blocks were dotted about the village. There was one, for example, in the gap between the two blocks of Caithness Row. The ubiquitous zinc bath was to be found in every house, but an unofficial public bath system also operated in the Dye Works, where an indulgent superintendent filled the great vats with water which would then be heated for the benefit of the villagers. The village Gasworks was supplanted by the coming of the electricity supply, but both were supposedly for lighting only. In each house hung just a single light bulb which was replaced by the Company, free of charge, when it burned out. The craftier villagers, however, soon found that it was possible to tap the electricity cable and operate such appliances as wirelesses and irons off the village supply. In an attempt at social control of which Owen would have approved, the electricity supply was switched off each evening at 11 and the village plunged into

*Colour plates on p. 25: **Left above**: No. 1 mill and, **below**, No. 3 mill. From **top right**: the mill lade; the Counting House, built by Owen, on the end of Caithness Row; Corra Linn; the village shop; the bell tower on New Buildings, transferred; from No. 1 mill in the mid-nineteenth century; Caithness Row.*

*Forgotten Years: The Company*
*A spinner at work; the traction engine which brought the cotton bales down to New Lanark; mill hands outside the Institute.*

*Forgotten Years: The Community Entering the village; the shop; Lanimers Day float: New Lanark took part in this traditional Lanark festival.*

*OtherTitles from MOUBRAY HOUSE PUBLISHING*

**THE ROYAL MILE: From Palace to Castle**
Author: Jim Crumley Photographs: Marius Alexander
Drawings: Richard Demarco ISBN 0 948473 14 2
A high quality illustrated volume which celebrates Scotland's most romantic way. Jim Crumley is a 'Scottish Feature Writer of the Year' and author of *St Kilda*; Marius Alexander is an award-winning photographer.
Price: £12.95 + £1.50 p&p hardback

**THE ROYAL BOTANIC GARDEN OF EDINBURGH BOOK OF THE SCOTTISH GARDEN**
Photographs: Brinsley Burbridge Text: Fay Young
ISBN 0 948473 12 6
Over 50 of Scotland's finest public and private gardens portrayed in a series of beautiful colour photographs commissioned by the Royal Botanic Garden.
Price: £19.95 + £2 p&p hardback

**FOOD FOR ALL SEASONS: IN SCOTLAND**
Modern Scottish Cooking ISBN 0 948473 10 X
Modern Scottish cooking arranged seasonally: in glorious colour. Four food writers, including Neil MacLean of The Sunday Times; family cooking, edible plants of the countryside, traditional fare updated. Recipes from Scotland's most creative cooks and chefs.
Price £12.95 + £1.50 p&p hardback

**W. WESTHOFEN: THE FORTH BRIDGE**
ISBN 0 948473 11 8
Centenary Edition: £27 Collector's Edition: £47 p&p £3

**A PICTURE HISTORY OF THE FORTH BRIDGE**
ISBN 0 948473 13 4
A photographic history tracing the construction of the world's most famous railway bridge.
Price to be announced.

**THE SCOTTISH INTERIORS CALENDAR 1990**
12 of the most popular houses included in the 'Scottish Interiors Series' in a high quality large format 'art' calendar.
Price: £5.95 + 50p p&p With cardboard sleeve for posting

**A LOCAL HISTORY SERIES** which portrays outstanding sites in Scotland. Fully illustrated in black & white and colour.
Each volume price: £2.50 + 50p p&p

**THE WILD FRONTIER: SCOTLAND'S ROMAN WALL**
Walking the Antonine Wall
Text: Anne Johnstone Introduced by Magnus Magnusson
ISBN 0 948473 03 7
A valuable and entertaining guide to Scotland's most important Roman monument.

**FACES OF LEITH**
Text: Sheila Mackay ISBN 0 948473 01 0
A fitting archive of Edinburgh's port.

**SILVER HIGHWAY: The Story of the Forth Road Bridge**
Text: Sheila Mackay and Fay Young ISBN 0 948473 09 6
25th Anniversary publication. Companion to 'Bridge Across the Century'.

**BRIDGE ACROSS THE CENTURY: The Story of the Forth Bridge**
Text: Sheila Mackay ISBN 0 948473 00 2
The vividly told story of the construction of Scotland's greatest historic engineering triumph.

**SCOTTISH INTERIORS SERIES**
Four full colour volumes covering four centuries of interior style represented by houses of major importance. Produced in association with the National Trust for Scotland.

'. . . high quality colour . . . puts Scotland on the interiors map'
The Scotsman

Price: £2.95 + £1 p&p each volume; £11.80 + £1 for the set of four

| | |
|---|---|
| **Scottish Renaissance Interiors** | ISBN 0 948473 06 1 |
| **Scottish Georgian Interiors** | ISBN 0 948473 05 3 |
| **Scottish Victorian Interiors** | ISBN 0 948473 04 5 |
| **Scottish Edwardian Interiors** | ISBN 0 948473 07 X |

**All these publications are available from bookshops throughout Scotland. Individual orders are available by post directly from: Moubray House Publishing Ltd., Tweeddale Court, 14 High Street, Edinburgh EH1 1TE. Telephone: 031 557 3349**

**Payment by ACCESS or VISA card or cheque.**

*An early photographic view of the village, probably dating from the 1880's. The burnt-out remains of No. 4 mill are still visible.*

*"20th February, 1883. Fire broke out in the 5th room of No. 4 mill this morning about 12.00 o'clock. Two men were working there levelling up the new mules and were using a naked light. The flames were first seen inside the carriage of the mule they were working at, and the course of the flames was away from them not towards them. The mill was burned to the ground."—* Works Manager's Report.

20 Feb 1883. Fire broke out in the 5th room of No 4 Mill this Morning about 12. O'clock. Two men were working there levelling up the new Mules, and were using a naked light, the flames were first seen inside the Carriage of the Mule they were working at and the Course of the flames was away from them, not towards them, the Mill was burned to the ground

*The combination of timber construction, the use of naked lights, highly flammable raw material and the friction of constantly moving machinery was lethal. Every mill in New Lanark, except No. 2, was at some stage during its working life, burnt to the ground: No. 1 in 1788, No. 3 in 1819 and No. 4 in 1883. Concern for fire prevention accounted for the importance attached to safer cast-iron building techniques when these became available, and the rebuilt No. 3 mill is a good example of such construction.*

*"25th July 1883. In 1st mill 3rd room at 11.45 Cathren Dods droped a flyer between the cylinders. She put her hand in to take it out and she received a sore bruise on the arm. It turns out that her arm is broken."*

25th July 1883 in 1st mill 3rd Room at 11.45 Cathren Dods Droped a flyer betwen the Cylinders. She put her hand in to take it out & She received a sore bruise on the arm it turns out that her arm is broken

*Even with a caring management, a cotton mill was, inevitably, a dangerous place. Most workers at New Lanark remember accidents. One mill hand recalls her father's grisly description of a woman, hair caught in the machinery, who was completely scalped. She managed to stagger into the canteen, the top of her head a bloody mass. Another remembers her uncle being sent off by the Company to learn to write with his left hand after all the fingers of his right had been taken off by a belt.*

darkness until 4 the following morning. However, concessions were made. Lights remained on in the case of serious illness or imminent childbirth.

Furniture was sparse and, for the most part, purely functional. Rooms had two "set in" (box) beds in each of which four children might sleep. Clothes were dried on an internal or external pulley and every home was provided with a "Company dresser" in which the family crockery would be kept. The cold flagstone floors were covered with linoleum but villagers still remember freezing nights which compelled them to huddle around the range.

Medical facilities of the community were provided by a doctor who, although not resident in New Lanark, kept a surgery in the village. Several contributory schemes paid for both medical and dental services. Spiritual needs were the concern of a minister who lived in the New Buildings and, before the building of the church, held services there. The lack of a church until relatively late on and of a Manse at any time during New Lanark's history was an interesting legacy of Owen's distinctly unenthusiastic attitude towards organised religion and both his predecessor's and successor's religious non-conformity.

## A GAME FOR EVERY SEASON

In the 1880s the village children were moved into a new school building at the top of the hill and the original school was left behind. With this innovation many of the elements of Owen's educational approach, including the dancing classes which had persisted right up to this period, disappeared. The old school building was eventually taken over by the Company for the finishing work which was required in net manufacturing. A mill hand who worked there sadly recalls the careless destruction of equipment and teaching aids which had been left over from previous decades.

FOR SALE, BY PRIVATE BARGAIN.

THE COTTON MILLS, &c., at New Lanark. These Works, so well known to the inhabitants of Great Britain, are situated within a mile of the Town of Lanark, and in the proximity of the Station of the Caledonian Railway, and are about 25 miles distant from Glasgow.

The Mills, which are four in number, contain—
22,800 Throstle Spindles,
28,900 Mule Spindles, Self actors, by Messrs. Sharp & Roberts,
13,000 Hand-Mule Spindles,
with all the necessary Preparation Machinery.

There is also an extensive Foundry and Mechanic Shop, containing the most modern and suitable Machinery and Tools.

There is also a large Store fitted up with everything necessary for the Sale of Grocery Goods and Cloths, and whatever is needful for the wants of the Workers.

There is also an excellent Gas Work for supplying the Works and the Village.

There is besides a large Building admirably fitted for the Educational purposes of the Village, and, in it, a commodious Hall used as a place of Worship, and capable of holding upwards of a thousand persons.

Connected with the Works, is the Village of New Lanark, capable of accommodating upwards of 2000 inhabitants, present population about 1700; and the Rental of which, with Stores and Gas, is upwards of £1400 per annum.

The Machinery of the Four Mills and Mechanic Shop is driven by Nine Water Wheels in all, equal to about 400 Horse Power, but which may be increased according to the wishes of the Proprietors.

There is, behind the main body of the Mills, the necessary Blowing Houses. Under the roof of the back Premises is a Cotton Cellar, capable of holding upwards of 300 Bales.

Adjoining the Village, is a Stone Quarry and Sand Pits, belonging to the Proprietors.

The whole Land, including the site of the Works and the Village, is about 225 Acres Imperial, of these there are about 206 Acres Arable and in Gardens and Wood.

The Feu-Duty on the whole Property is £96, and the Public Burdens are very moderate.

In the immediate neighbourhood of the Mills is the most sublime scenery in Scotland, or even in Great Britain. It is almost needless to mention the magnificent Falls of the Clyde and the stupendous Cartland Craigs, with the beautiful Landscape of the Vale of Clyde. In short, Cotton Works more suited to the conducting, on an extensive scale, the Cotton Spinning Business, from the immediate application of the Water Power to the Machinery, or the capability of extending the Machinery is not to be found in any other part of the Island.

Every facility, with regard to the terms of payment of the purchase money, will be given.

The Works may be seen at any time, on application to the present Proprietors resident there.

New Lanark, 8th February, 1851.

*In 1851 the Walkers attempted to sell New Lanark and placed this advertisement in the Glasgow Herald. No purchaser was found and the village remained in their ownership for a further 30 years.*

"Every season had its game," says one villager, recalling her childhood in New Lanark. There were the games played everywhere in the area – Sheep Lie Low, Buff the Bear, Gird and Cleek, Harry Lee, Hunch Cuddy Hunch – and also those which lent themselves to an uncrowded village: fishing and paddling in the Clyde, skipping, marbles, bowls and peevers in the vehicle-free streets. There were games, too, which emphasised the distinctiveness of the community: Whuppity Scourie, for instance, when the boys of Old and New Lanark fought it out:

*"Hooray boys, hooray*
*We've won the day!*
*We've beat the bold Old Lanark boys*
*And chased them up the Brae!"*

So cried the triumphant New Lanarkians on those occasions when the invasion had been routed and the Lanark youngsters had beaten a hasty retreat up the hill to their homes.

For adults and children alike there were the memories of the annual holidays: ten days in August spent by the sea at Portobello or Ayr or, for workers with Irish relations, in the hills of County Down or on Orange Marches through stern, but bunting-lined, Ulster streets. Holidaymakers came in great numbers to New Lanark, too: no longer to view the works of Dale or Owen but once again to enjoy the beauties of the Falls of Clyde. Village children picked flowers to sell to them or, less scrupulously, took advantage of their own barefooted state – shoes were for winter only – to beg. One small girl returning home with her dubiously acquired booty was confronted by an understandably displeased mother. The child refused to feel any sense of shame. Clutching her thruppenny bit, she remembers, "I thought I was Carnegie."

The Institute remained the focus of social life for the adults of the village. Here it was that they held their dances – sometimes returning to bed at 3 or 4 in the morning to rise again in time for work at 6 – played "carpet bowls", performed dramas and married. To the very end of the village's working life this building, whether known as the Institute or the Big Hall, provided many of the functions for which it had been intended when Robert Owen opened it in January, 1816.

SILENT MILLS

In September, 1967, all the employees of the Gourock Ropework Company at New Lanark were called to a meeting in the Institute. It was announced that the mills were to close immediately. The incredulous workers had had no inkling of the decision. There was a shocked silence: "You could have heard a pin drop." By March, 1968, the last processes had been completed. The bell atop New Buildings which had regulated the working day, brought in the New Year and announced Sunday services, rang no more. There were some aspects of the mill's passing which could not be regretted: the long hours, the heat, the sight of young girls emerging from work covered with the grease of machinery and the turkey-red dyes of the textiles – or looking like snowmen, the cotton dust of the preparation rooms clinging to them. Other workers found the atmosphere of a Company village – living in the shadow of their factory – distinctly claustrophobic. But the awareness of community and of a purpose behind the running of this manufacturing village – which went far beyond mere economic gain for the proprietors – existed to the end. If by the 1960s conditions in New Lanark were not so very different from those in similar communities elsewhere, it was hardly a sign of failure. New Lanark had not so much fallen behind; rather it was the rest of the world which had caught up.

# NEW LIFE FOR NEW LANARK

"It's no exaggeration to say that the setting up of the New Lanark Conservation Trust in 1975 was the last throw of the dice before the bulldozers moved in." Today it's difficult to reconcile the statement of Jim Arnold, New Lanark's Manager, with the view from the window of his office in Mill Three of scores of people at work on the restoration of the village. But it is indeed the case that New Lanark, now Clydesdale's star visitor attraction and one of only a few Scottish sites nominated for inclusion in the World Heritage list was, until recently, a prime candidate for demolition.

The half dozen or so years following the 1968 closure formed the darkest hour in New Lanark's colourful history. Before that, the Gourock Ropework Company had been at pains to improve housing conditions. In 1963 it helped to establish one of Scotland's first Housing Associations in the village. The Association, with a loan from Lanark Town Council, restored some 25 houses in Caithness Row and Nursery Buildings under the supervision of architects Ian Lindsay & Partners. It was a bold initiative which, at times after 1968, appeared to have been in vain. For two years after closure the mill buildings remained unused. The commercial balance between the advantages of water power and the disadvantages of remoteness, which had tipped the scales in Dale and Owen's favour, was gone. In the mid-twentieth century the potential of water power had become an irrelevance. All that New Lanark could offer an industrial purchaser was a vast floor space in an inaccessible rural setting.

*The School in 1972, after the collapse of its roof.*

Finally, in 1970, the mill buildings were sold to Metal Extractions Ltd., a reprocessing company, and for a short time there were hopes for new employment in the community. These were unfounded. Ugly mounds of scrap metal appeared in and around the mills and few local jobs were created. New Lanark's population, which had stood at 300 when the mills closed, eventually fell to 80. The Housing Association programme came to a standstill – the costs of rehabilitation, involving external as well as internal work, was too great to be contemplated. The Local Authority was becoming understandably concerned about the mounting size of the loan it had made, which with interest payments was now approaching £150,000.

In 1971, with something approaching desperation, Lanark Town Council and the Scottish Civic Trust convened a meeting at a Lanark hotel to discuss the problem. Harry Smith, the Provost of Lanark, was persuaded to take the chair, and has remained New Lanark's champion to this day as chairman firstly of the Working Party which was set up as a result of that meeting, then of New Lanark Trust and now of the reconstituted Conservation Trust. The discussions of the working party led in 1973 to the official paper, A *Future for New Lanark*, presented, as Jim Arnold notes with an historian's memory of Robert Owen's writings, as a second *Report to the County of Lanark*. It paved the way for, among other things, the appointment of New Lanark's Manager, whose post was to be funded jointly by the Historic Buildings Council for Scotland, Strathclyde Regional Council and Clydesdale District Council.

Looking back over the past decade-and-a-half, Graham U'ren, Clydesdale's Director of Planning, underlines the Local Authority's consistent support in the regeneration of New Lanark, but points out the two crucial factors in which changed the village's fortunes were the appointment of Jim Arnold as New Lanark's Manager and the involvement of the Manpower Services Commission.

Jim Arnold arrived in the village in 1974 from a career in industry and further education. The introduction to the job as Manager was hardly propitious. When he first arrived at his designated office in Robert Owen's Counting House he lacked even a key to open the door, and having finally gained entry, found the room had no electricity or telephone! It was at this time that Housing Association grants for the rehabilitation of the tenancies were curtailed. This at least cleared the way for purchaser-restorer schemes. In 1975, houses in Braxfield Row were the first to be sold, with strict conditions attached, to prospective restorers. For the first time in its history, New Lanark was to have its share of owner-occupied houses.

As if rewarding this bold initiative, fortune now began to favour the village. Housing legislation in the mid-70s lifted the burden of the loan from the local authority and, in 1976, help became available for the first time through the Manpower Services Commission. M.S.C. funded labour carried out restoration work to the external fabric of houses using building materials – stone, slates, roofing and flooring timbers –

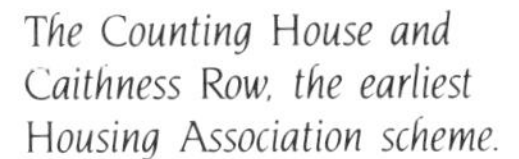
*The Counting House and Caithness Row, the earliest Housing Association scheme.*

1820

▲ (追)。 Owen's Reply to the Address
the Inhabitants of New Lanark.

容.]
19 年十一月末 New Lanark 工場の四大建物の一つ
ンで活躍してゐたオウエンは急遽歸り，その善後處
者愛護を敢行し彼らの『福祉への不斷の注意ぶり』を
nark 村民はこの事件と二十年來の施政への自ら湧き
てオウエンへの感謝狀を再び（前に一度したことがあ
，委員會を選任して 1820 年二月八日村民集會の決議
狀を，村民列席の下に New Institution である月
と。（委員長 Alexander Innes 書記長 George L. M
勞働者が勞働條件・Infant School 設備・燒失善後
の全人物全施政への "grateful acknowledgement'
の下院立候補の成功翹望を以て結んだこの感謝の會に
滿腔の愉悦だつたに相違ない。"FRIENDS, ASSOCIATE
とよびかけてはじまるこの Reply はむくいられた
に充ちてゐる。 二十年施政の追憶と成功。 自己の
"severe distress" が充滿してゐる工場地帶農村
を擴大すべき社會變革へむかつてすゝまんとし，先
をえんとしてする下院立候補の心境に及ぶ。 最後
vours shall be always exerted for their well-bei
村民に保證して終る。簡單ながらオウエン事業史中
[Bibliographical Description]

*One of the more intriguing New Lanark connections has been with Japan. Japanese visitors, fascinated by the close parallels between the philosophy and practice of Owenism in the village and their own 'company system' have been coming to New Lanark since the 1920s. In 1934 this interest prompted a Japanese professor, Shigeru Goto of Yokohama, to compile what has become the standard bibliography of Owenite literature. Japan now boasts the largest Robert Owen Society in the world. Masoko Shoji, Professor of Child Education at Hiroshima University, visited New Lanark in 1961, shortly after the elaborate celebrations held in Japan to mark the centenary of Owen's death.*

The Manpower Services Commission workforce – over 200 strong – was employed both in restoring the buildings and researching the history of the village.

Some 120,000 visitors now pour into New Lanark each year.

paid for jointly by the Historic Buildings Council for Scotland and the local authorities. Thus buildings were brought to a state where the rest of the works necessary for internal rehabilitation fell within the financial limits of the Housing Association. It now became feasible once again to consider the restoration of tenanted properties. Since then some 43 tenancies have been restored, with ten more planned. In addition 20 purchaser/restorer schemes have been completed in Braxfield and Long Rows and 11 more scheduled in the Rows. Most housing rehabilitation schemes have been to standard Housing Association requirements but one tenement at the end of Double Row was to be meticulously restored to its original condition by the Historic Buildings and Monuments Directorate of the Scottish Development Department and will become a "museum stair".

The emphasis up to this time had been on the restoration of housing. Now attention shifted to other buildings in the village. The roof of Owen's school had collapsed and was a particular cause for concern. This building and the others upstream from it were purchased by the district council in 1974 and under the direction of the S.D.D. work began on the restoration of the School. David Dale's and Robert Owen's houses were also purchased by the Housing Association from Metal Extractions Ltd. in 1978.

The problems surrounding the Institute and the mill buildings themselves were altogether greater, but the challenge of overcoming them was to prove a rallying catalyst for the various bodies involved in the regeneration of the village. In 1979 Clydesdale District Council, alarmed by the continuing deterioration of the mill buildings, served a Repairs Notice on Metal Extractions Ltd. In 1983 it compulsorily purchased the buildings. It was a brave move – the first time that legislation had been used in this way to secure the future of historic buildings in Scotland – only made possible through the National Heritage Memorial Fund which underwrote the purchase cost. The constitution of New Lanark Conservation Trust was subsequently altered to allow it to acquire the buildings.

Work is in progress on a permanent visitor centre in the Institute and Mill Three. The development potential of this project, due to be completed in 1990, has brought a number of other organisations into the picture. The Scottish Development Agency has cleared the formerly scrap-laden ground around the mills and funded a Development Officer's post. The Scottish Tourist Board has grant-aided the building of a car park for visitors. The Countryside Commission for Scotland has helped the Scottish Wildlife Trust to establish an exhibition in the former workshops at the far end of the village.

The contributions of all of these and other bodies are acknowledged on a large board which Jim Arnold has hung in a prominent position. At times, when this long list brings to mind the complicated funding relationships involved in the creation of the new New Lanark, Jim sighs and dreams of the simplicity of co-operating with a single backer. The outsider, on the other hand, cannot help admiring the variety of ideas and relative independence which such a range of sponsors has produced. There is also, it must be admitted, a certain historical satisfaction in seeing the present day Manager of New Lanark working with numerous partners to such imaginative ends – much in the manner of his most distinguished predecessor, Robert Owen.

*The inhabitants of New Lanark in 1985. From a lowpoint of 80, the population has grown to 100 and, it is planned, will eventually rise to some 300 people.*

*Harry Smith **(centre)** and Jim Arnold **(right)** join in a toast to mark the restoration of the bell tower; another step towards the revival of New Lanark.*